GAME OF GODS

i *to* I

ALCYONÉ SUMILA STARR

Published in the United States of America

Brilliant Books Literary
137 Forest Park Lane Thomasville
North Carolina 27360 USA

ISBN:
Paperback: 979-8-88945-497-7
Ebook: 979-8-88945-498-4
Hardback: 979-8-88945-499-1

Contents

ACKNOWLEDGEMENT

The credit goes to you Gladiator, my divine friend, for introducing me to my non-physical True Self.

DEDICATION

This book is dedicated to Leshma for her unwavering conviction that I would, one day, shine a light on the path, that could free humanity from suffering.

INTRODUCTION

This book "'i' to 'I': Game of Gods" is a sequel to my books–
YOU ARE THE ULTIMATE MAGICIAN: Fearlessly create the life of your dreams.

YOU ARE THE ULTIMATE MAGICIAN: Know thy power and be free–Book 2

YOU ARE THE ULTIMATE MAGICIAN: Love–the final frontier-Book 3.

This trilogy was about Maxim de Winter, a billionaire entrepreneur famously known around the world as Gladiator, the spiritual teacher. Although he was considered to have supernatural powers, he never accepted it. He declared every human is born with the power to create his desired reality.

In this book, Maxim de Winter jr., twenty years young son of Gladiator and Alaska de Winter, talks about his interpretation of the spiritual laws as taught by his parents to him.

Maxim jr. takes the readers step by step through the spiritual process. He explains in detail what is this 'love' he talks about and why only 'love' will do. He goes on to show how to generate, harness and use the magical power of 'love' to free humanity from suffering.

He states, as did Gladiator, to be a happy master creator you need to raise your vibration to the frequency of love, the frequency of your non-physical True Self.

This book is very relevant to current day problems of conflict and chaos around the world. People are discouraged and disheartened. Their pessimistic mind set can be changed by a new way of life.

How to use the power of 'love', is explained in this book, as a measure for effecting a paradigm shift in consciousness by leading from the heart instead of the head. I hope you will use the spiritual teachings in this book for the purpose.

Afterall everyone is looking for a happier life free of suffering!

Alcyoné Sumila Starr.

PREFACE

There is a reason why this book is in your hands, my friends. There always is, believe me.

Although this book has been published under the genre of spiritual fiction, in truth, it is a Self-help book par excellence! I would like to remind you that the text of this book is indeed alive with the transforming power of the Creator.

So, what is the best way to read this book? For the first read, if you are interested in the story, you may like to read the book as fast as you can, but then you need to follow it at a slower pace. This slower pace will help you absorb the vibration of the words. Certain words, phrases and spiritual practices have been purposely repeated under different headings so that the spiritual truths go deep in your sub-conscious mind. Slowly it will bring the desired change in your mental and physical system for your highest good.

May the Force of Love be with you!

Alcyoné Sumila Starr

CHAPTER 1

Maxim De Winter Jr. Comes

THERE WAS ANTICIPATION in the air, a silent unspoken excitement on their faces. One could sense the expectation of the uncommon, the miraculous, the magical, or something mystical to happen. The crowd could hardly contain its impatience at the delay. It did not want to miss a single moment out of the long-awaited visit of the man, or shall we call him the boy, he is after all only twenty years of age.

Let me introduce you to Maxim de Winter Jr., son of Maxim de Winter, billionaire entrepreneur and Alaska de Winter. His father was more famously known as Gladiator, the spiritual teacher. He was said to have supernatural powers. He could see through the veil of life and death. His sheer presence could transform people.

So, approximately five years ago, the world was shocked to hear and could hardly believe that Gladiator, with his wife Alaska, was lost while flying to an island, leaving behind their son under the guardianship of their friends Brian and Mark.

On continued demand of the spiritual community around the world, to meet Maxim de Winter Jr., Gladiator's spiritual school agreed to arrange this seminar for the purpose.

To look at the crowd, one is justified in wondering at the chief attraction for this huge gathering. As far as I know no one has met the boy. At a guess I think it is his unusual pedigree. His grandmother Angelina, his great uncle Martin, his father Gladiator and his mother Alaska all were steeped into spirituality. Anyways it is said the boy, Maxim Jr., is very different from us mortals!

So, let us wait patiently for him to arrive. It is already past his scheduled arrival time of 5PM. I can see the organizers standing in front of the huge door to welcome him. But there is no sign of the boy. Where is he? Is he even coming? Oh, wait, there is some commotion at the door. The organizers looked surprised and rushed into the auditorium.

Well, what do you think happened? Hold your heart my friends. It seems Maxim Jr. arrived out of the blue, so to speak, straight on the stage. He does not need a car to come to the seminar like us common people. Oh, I think it is going to be interesting listening to this futuristic boy.

Well, there is complete silence in the hall. Every eye is fixed on the tall young man grinning at the crowd waiting for the organizers to reach the stage. He does look like Gladiator—handsome, attractive with same indigo eyes but that is where the resemblance ends. He has laughing indigo eyes while Gladiator had intense piercing indigo eyes, that unnerved most people when he looked at them. It is rumored that in seconds, Gladiator could read a roomful of people like open books. It is true this young man has the same indigo-colored eyes, but he has a different kind of palpable energy around him. It appears as if he cannot contain his joy. He seems to be literally glowing with some inner light. We have heard so much about extra-ordinary powers of his parents that I wonder if Maxim Jr. is indeed present here or if I am seeing some kind of holographic reflection of the boy.

Mr. Prentice, the chief organizer, with his secretary finally reached the stage. He looked stunned. He asked "Mr. de Winter? How did you come? We were waiting outside for you."

Maxim de Winter Jr. smiled a little sheepishly and replied "I got delayed at the school. If I had waited for the car, I would have been late for this seminar, so I opted to come on my own. I hope you do not mind."

It took the welcoming committee couple of minutes to recover from the shock of his sudden appearance on the stage. After a minute or so Mr. Prentice replied "No, no, Mr. de Winter. You are more than welcome. We have been looking forward to meeting you for the last five years."

Maxim Jr. asked softly "Really?"

Mr. Prentice rushed to confirm "Yes, yes, it is the truth Mr. de Winter. We were only surprised a little at your mode of conveyance."

Maxim Jr. said with a big grin "Sorry, you did not like my mode of conveyance. Mr. Prentice I was talking about the reason you wanted me to come here. The truth, as I understand, is that you wished to recreate the magic of my parents' presence, but I regret I cannot fulfill it."

Mr. Prentice interrupted him "But you have young man, you have! Believe me! Your parents' sudden departure left us aching for some communication. We felt bereft of their benevolent presence. You are our link to them! I wonder if you know how much you look like your father."

Junior murmured "Do I?"

After a short pause he said "Well, maybe, if you say so, but does it matter? What difference can I make in anyone's life?"

Mr. Prentice replied with a smile "Mr. de Winter, it does! You do. Your presence does exactly what your parents did.

You are radiating something, I don't know what, that is energizing everything in the auditorium! I feel it. We all feel it!"

Hearing him Junior threw back his head and laughed out loud. He asked "Really? Well, then my work is done. Can I go home now?"

"No" there was a roar from the audience.

Mr. Prentice said with a smile "There is your answer".

Junior scratched his head and asked with his usual grin "Well then what would you like me to do?

"Tell me how to effortlessly create my dream world literally out of thin air" said a girl standing near the side entrance to the hall.

Junior turned to look at her. He went silent when he saw her emerald-green eyes. Could she be his green eyed one? He stared for a few seconds, then shook his head disappointed. He said "Well, your Gladiator has already explained it in detail. Spiritual truths do not change. In any case I am not a teacher. I am a student myself. Every day I learn something new, and I enjoy experimenting, specially, with higher frequencies and dimensions."

Junior looked at the audience and continued "Please do contact our spiritual school. We have the best teachers. They will tell you how you can create your dream world. They will explain why Gladiator called you ultimate magicians and they will also explain anything else you want to know about."

Junior paused and looked around.

A lady sitting in the front row said "Yes, we know about Gladiator's spiritual school. We do use it and are grateful for it but today, believe it or not, today we are here to see you, to hear you, to know you Mr. Maxim de Winter Jr.! You were privileged to have such brilliant parents. You must have absorbed some of that brilliance. Won't you share it with us?"

Junior nodded and then went still with his unblinking indigo eye wide open.

There was pin drop silence in the hall. No one moved. The audience waited patiently for Maxim Jr. to come back to the present, back to them.

After a minute of silence Junior blinked his eyes and said with a smile "Yes, there is this thing, I learned from my parents which no one talks about in connection with spirituality. I hope you will forgive me if it does not come up to your expectation. It is quite simple. I can sum it up in one word– 'Love', love for no reason!"

Junior looked around expectantly but didn't get any reaction from the audience. So, he waited some more.

CHAPTER 2

What is Love?

"YES, THAT IS it "Junior repeated" I learned from my brilliant parents to love, to feel love unconditionally, and be full of joy."

Junior looked around the hall again. The audience remained silent.

He smiled ruefully and turned towards Mr. Prentice. He asked "Er..do I have your permission to leave now?"

That question suddenly brought the audience awake. There was a kind of general commotion in the hall.

Junior turned towards them. With a twinkle in his eyes, he asked "Did you have a question after all?"

His question was met with complete chaos. Hundreds of people were speaking at the same time. There was complete pandemonium in the hall till Mr. Prentice roared "Silence!" That did the trick. The audience calmed down and became quiet.

Mr. Prentice pointed to an elderly gentleman sitting in the first row and asked "Sir, do you have a question for Mr. de Winter? If yes, please ask now, and all others kindly remain quiet."

The man replied "Yes, I have a question. Can I call you Maxim?"

"Yes, sure, you can. Why not call me Junior instead of Maxim? Everyone does at home. When you say Mr.de Winter I start looking around for my father." Replied Junior with a laugh.

"Alright then, Junior, you summed up all that you learned from your parents in one word, that is LOVE. Well, obviously you understood what they meant by love, but we do not! Could you explain what is this love you all talk about? And then, why love? Is it the answer to all our problems? And, lastly how to use this love and be free from suffering."

Junior, standing alone under the spotlight on the stage, genuinely looked surprised at the question. He murmured "Really? Really you don't understand love. Please give me a moment."

He paused for a few seconds running his fingers through his thick hair and then with a laugh he began "Love that we talk about is beyond the comprehension of logical mind, so I will not even try to define it. But love gives meaning to life. Love cannot be limited. It is like a wide-open space ready to embrace all, without judgement, as our Creator does. It is also the Divine Life Force. It gives life to the creation. It is the glue that keeps our limitless Universe in place, ticking away and expanding in space. No, it is not just an emotion. Seers and saints said God is love. It is said our Creator loved us into existence. So, it follows, anything you love unconditionally, will come to life. Didn't your Gladiator encouraged you to raise your vibration to the frequency of love and become the master creator you were meant to be? Guess what–you are floating in this unseen omnipresent ocean of love, loved, cherished and pampered, and yet you remain unaware of it! Surprising, isn't it? By overlooking love, our analytical mind could have reasoned it out of your life and thus, could have succeeded in depriving humanity of its power! Your heart, your soul is filled with so much of love from the Creator that you can never ever be lonely! You need to learn to experience it. What do you say?"

In unison the audience yelled "Yes"!

Junior laughed and continued "I hope I was able to give you, at least, some idea about the magnificence of 'love'. Although I cannot define it but, all the same, I shall give you some pointers for recognizing it. Let me relate a story my mother used to tell her audience. This is how she had replied, when her father had asked her if she loved Maxim, my father, before they got married. He had asked 'You love him Little one?' and she had replied 'Dad I really don't know. I only know that I am happy because Maxim is in my life.' So, you see, you can recognize love when you feel happy just because she/he/it is in your life. Her/his/its sheer presence in your life is enough for you to be joyous. No other reason is required for it. You do not expect her/him/it to change in anyway to please you or you don't hold him/her responsible for your happiness."

Junior with a big grin continued "In short, love is that something, that unseen essence that you feel in your heart. It encompasses the beauty of your passion, your compassion, your joy, your kindness, your gratitude and all things good. It is priceless. It cannot be bought or sold but is free for you, if you are ready for it! How is that?"

Junior laughed and repeated "How is that? Remember, it is totally free! Want some?"

The audience were enjoying his questions and said "Yes."

Junior sobered up and said "Do you remember your Gladiator used to say–'Love is our final frontier. So, we must be consciously aware of our final frontier, this boundless loving intelligence we are made-out-of. And how can we do that?-Simply by stopping our thoughts for a couple of seconds! And feel. What you feel is the unseen essence of your True self, that is the 'love' we talk about!

Junior stopped and said "Sorry Mr. Prentice, I need to go now. I have taken too long. My guardian would be waiting for me."

Then he looked at the audience and said "Your next question was WHY love. Next weekend I will explain it. Please contact the spiritual school they will arrange everything."

Mr. Prentice asked "How are you going, same way you came? My car will drop you home."

Junior grinned and replied "Oh no, Brian would have sent the car with all security in place, to keep me safe, so to speak. Thank you. I enjoyed it."

He waved his hands once again and jumped from the stage and ran out of the hall before the audience could start clapping.

CHAPTER 3

Enter-Brian and Mark–guardians of Maxim de Winter Jr.

MARK, A HANDSOME man in early forties, was sitting in a well-appointed stylish room sipping tea while perusing some documents. He had an unusual aura of peace around him.

Mark was Junior's mother, Alaska's college friend. Gladiator and Alaska had appointed him Junior's guardian in the event of their untimely death.

Brian, a friend of Gladiator, was the other guardian for Junior who managed the vast business empire of De Winter Enterprises for him.

Mark heard the front door open and the brisk steps of Brian coming in the room. The moment he saw Mark he asked, "Where is he?" He sounded exasperated.

Mark replied with a smile "Relax, have some tea, Brian. He should be here soon."

Brian retorted "It is easy for you to say that. You do not face the chief security officer of De Winter Enterprises' complaining and blaming me for Junior's reckless actions. Do you know what he did today? He was supposed to be at the seminar at 5 PM but when I checked he was still busy in his laboratory! When he saw me, he quickly said, 'sorry Brian' and teleported or whatever he does, straight to the seminar leaving behind his jacket as well as his guards. He doesn't bother about his own safety, but I am responsible for it. Between the security chief and Junior, I will become a nervous reck!"

Mark looked at Brian and calmly asked "Do you really think anyone can harm Junior? No, it can only happen if, for some reason, Junior wants to experience it, and God forbid if he does, we would not be able to do anything about it."

Mark took a sip of tea and said "Brian, I don't think he will, because he knows it will hurt both of us. The child cares for us, believe it or not. So, let us enjoy our tea and await his arrival."

Brian looked up at the painting over the fireplace. It was a beautiful painting done by Gladiator himself of his wife, Alaska, Junior's mother. The painting seemed alive. Alaska's dazzling smile made Brian forget the world. He kept looking at it till tears came to his eyes. He was not sure if the tears were for losing her first to his friend, Maxim, or now, to eternity.

He came to the present when he heard Junior running into the room.

"Hey Brian, I am home, all safe and sound. Mark what are you drinking? I am hungry. What is there to eat?" asked Junior.

Mark smiled and replied "Come Junior let us go to the dining room and find out what is laid out for you to eat. Don't forget to wash your hands first."

Junior grinned and said "Yes, I will Mark. Hey Brian, are you still annoyed with me for forgetting to go to the seminar on time? You need not have worried as I was on the stage at

5.01 PM. Truly, except the audience was struck dumb by my sudden presence on the stage. Oh, Mark it was so funny!"

Saying that he ran to wash his hands whistling some jaunty tune.

Brian looked at Mark and they burst out laughing.

Junior was back in seconds and sat down to eat. He looked at Mark and said "Guess what happened? Now that I come to think of it, it was comical. Mr. Prentice, poor man, took couple of minutes to recover from the shock of my presence on the stage and then he welcomed me. He said for the past 5 years he has been waiting to meet me. I wonder. Anyways after a couple of minutes I asked him, now that we have met, can I go home? But then a girl from the audience asked me to explain how to create a dream world out of thin air. I said I was not a teacher. She should contact the Spiritual school and ask them. Anyway, to cut the long story short I was finally asked to share something special that I might have learned from my parents. That was easy to answer. I told them it could be summed up in one word, that is, 'love.' This pronouncement of mine was met with complete silence. After waiting for a minute or so, I again asked Mr. Prentice if now, I could go home. Mark, can you guess what happened then"?

Mark smiled and said "No, I cannot guess. What happened then?"

Brian said "Oh, of course I can guess Junior. They asked you what you mean by love, the million-dollar question. So, what did you do?"

Junior replied "Brian you are a spoilsport. Well, they asked me 3 questions. First-what is this love we talk about. Second-Why only love and the third–how to use this love."

Mark quizzed him, "So, did you tell them something about love or dodged it?"

Junior replied with a grin "No, I didn't dodge. I told them about love, as I know it, but......."

Brian asked, "But what?"

"Mmm, I wonder if they got it. If they grasped the true meaning of the word 'love' and also, that it is the essence of our True self." Replied Junior.

Mark replied "Don't doubt my son. Take it from me, they got it, they got, as much as they were ready for."

Junior brightened up and exclaimed "Do you think so? Anyways, so today I talked about 'what is love' and took my leave after promising to talk about 'Why love' next week on our school video so everyone can watch."

CHAPTER 4

Why Love

MAXIM DE WINTER jr., handsome young man laughing with twinkling indigo eyes came into view on the screen.

He waved his hands and said with a grin "Here I am! I know you thought I will not come. But I came because I do want to share with you some of the knowledge I learned from my parents.

So, your second question was 'Why Love?'.

Because-

LOVE is the difference between-

Heaven and hell

Divinity and humanity

Beauty and ugliness

Joy and suffering

Health and sickness

Success and failure

Abundance and lack.

Etc.Etc. Etc....

In short, you will never feel whole and complete and balanced if you do not re-learn to 'love', and, also re-awaken yourself to feel love. You may achieve name, fame and success in this 3D reality, but you will not be satisfied with it. You will continue looking for that un-namable something outside of you for that illusive satisfaction.

You see love is the mystery behind the magic that transforms. You have heard of Philosopher's stone, haven't you? Any base metal turns to gold when touched by it. Anything, everything when touched by love transforms into its highest version.

Love is the essence of creation. Without love your life would be like a rose garden without the fragrance of rose. Life won't be worth living.

It is common practice to give least importance to love. It is supposed to be, relevant only to teenage romantic girls or emotional women, not for honest hard working respected people who do everything with the attitude of duty. Alas, they don't know what they are depriving themselves of! 'Love' is our true power!

Main challenge with the 'love', I am talking about, is that your mind cannot understand it. It is beyond its capability. But, although your head cannot comprehend love, the good news is, you can feel it in your heart, and you don't need another person or thing to feel it.

You can see the power of 'love', in action, by using it as a mantra in your daily life. You can repeat silently 'I love you' or 'I love myself' or "I am love' or any other phrase that resonates with you. In a couple of weeks, you would be surprised to feel the change in your life!

To cut the long story short, to create anything, to give life to any idea, to your vision, you need this magical power of love. It is possible to create anything if you can love it!

Now you know 'Why Love'."

Junior laughed and paused for a short while.

"I wonder if I made it clear to all of you why love is so important for us to know. If you have further questions about it, please contact our spiritual school. I repeat, we have best teachers to help you."

Junior continued "Your third question was 'How to use love'. Next week I will endeavor to explain it at the same time, same place!"

With his usual grin and a wave of his hands he went off the air.

As he was leaving the stage, he heard someone calling, "Mr. de Winter?"

He stopped and looked back with raised eyebrows...

CHAPTER 5

Fear Stops Here

"**M**R. DE WINTER?**"** again called Rita, the project technician.

Junior looked at her, without replying, with his eyebrows raised.

Rita giggled and amended "Okay, Junior, do you have a moment free?"

Junior grinned and said, "Well, I can make a moment free for you, if we can have a cappuccino in the café during that free moment. Okay with you?"

Rita said, "Yes, let us go. It won't take long. You see I read a quote from a Zen master which intrigued me. It goes something like this. 'If you can love your enemy, you will never have an enemy in your life ever again.' Is it possible Junior?"

Junior said, "Anything is possible if you can believe it Rita, but I think you wanted to ask 'how' one can love his/her enemy. Right?"

Rita laughed and said, "Yes, you are right. How can one love the enemy?"

Junior said, "You see you have 'free-will'. You are free to choose how you wish to perceive a person or a thing. You can choose to perceive the world through a lens of love or joy or peace, or fear or anger. Yes, the list goes on for you to choose from.

Now, your feelings about anyone or anything depends on the meaning you assign to it. Have you heard of someone loving the rain and someone hating the same rain? You see, their analytical mind gives them reason to like or dislike the rain. Their mind made the choice for them, and they started feeling good or bad depending on the meaning assigned to it. Is it clear Rita?"

"Yes, please go ahead."

Junior continued, "But, the people have the power to change the meaning they, or their mind, gave to the behavior of the other man, that had made them decide he was an enemy. When they change the meaning, they change their feelings. If, somehow, they came to know that it was a misunderstanding or that he was in too much of pain or something like that, your feeling would change to compassion towards your erstwhile enemy!"

He took a sip of his coffee and continued, "As per the quote of the Zen master, you know the obvious benefit of loving your enemy. So, if you wish to have the benefit, you could consciously change your thought, and its meaning, and thus would succeed in changing your feeling about the person, without trying to find any reason to do so."

"Rita, there is another thing to note here. When you feel love, you obviously vibrate at the high frequency of love, and when you vibrate at the frequency of love you cannot consider anyone as your enemy. You perceive everyone through the lens of love. Got it?" asked Junior.

"I think so." She replied.

"Let me give you another example." Junior said, "Let us take 'fear.' If you can love 'fear', fear will never trouble you again. Okay, so how can you love 'fear'? Again, by changing your thoughts about 'fear', or the thing you fear, or the circumstances you fear. Everything you perceive is created by you, and created for a reason, and believe me, the reason is always to help you." So now, you got the reason–'to help you', the new meaning you could assign to 'fear'.

Junior took a few more sips of his coffee and with a laugh he continued, "So, when you feel 'fear', embrace it with loving gratitude, for being there 'to help you'. Feel the loving gratitude in your heart! Do not shrink away from 'fear', do not feel constricted. Open your heart wide and embrace it with love. That is when 'fear' stops!"

Junior smiled and said, "When 'love' enters, 'fear' exits! But it must be your conscious choice. What will it be Rita? Would you prefer to carry on thinking thoughts and beliefs about 'fear', and feel fear, or would you deliberately choose to change it to thoughts about 'love', and feel love and enjoy the power of love?

And, of course, there is the high frequency of love to consider. When you feel love, you vibrate at the frequency of love. 'Fear' and shades of fear vibrate at a much lower frequency. They get dissolved in the frequency of love."

Junior paused and asked with a grin, "Does it make any sense, Rita? Practice it. Be the master of your thoughts."

"Yes, I will, and now I do understand the quote of the Zen master. Thank you, Junior. You are a genius!" Rita said.

"Am I?" said Junior and laughed out loud.

CHAPTER 6

Mom Chose Dad

JUNIOR BOUNDED UP couple of steps into De Winter Enterprises building and up the elevator on to his room or rather the room his father had used when he was alive. He looked at the painting of his mother, Alaska, hanging on the wall for quite some time. Then he blew a kiss at the painting and said "Love you Mom". He picked up the framed photo of his father that he kept on the big mahogany table and said "Love you, Dad. Thank you for painting this picture of Mom."

He went out and asked the receptionist "Where is Brian?"

"Mr. Brian is in the meeting Mr. de Winter." She replied.

"What, still in the meeting? That is not acceptable. Which room he is in?" Junior asked.

With a smile she replied, "In the third meeting hall Mr. de Winter."

With his usual grin he said, "Let me get him out of the meeting."

He knocked once at the door and walked in the room where a dozen or, so people were busy in some discussion.

He said "Good evening gentlemen. I regret but I must take Brian away now. Doctor's order you see!"

Everyone responded with "Good evening Mr. de Winter."

Brian said "Wait Junior. Let me finish this. It will take just a few minutes…."

Junior laughed and with a flick of his fingers made the pen from Brian's hand fly to his own hand. Everyone was amused. They were quite used to his antics. Junior pulled Brian's chair and said "Come Brian, Doctor said you need rest and rest you will! You work too hard. You need rest. Robert, Mr. Delaney please take care of his work. I promise he will be back tomorrow morning to sort out any remaining problem. Thank you."

Brian walked with Junior mumbling "Junior you do not understand the urgency of this work. I had to finalize it today."

Junior winked at Robert and replied with a grin "De Winter Enterprises will prosper till it is needed by the people. Brian, you do know it has its own life?"

He looked at the receptionist and asked her "Hasn't Mark come?"

"Yes, he just walked in. He is waiting in your room Mr. De Winter."

Junior with Brian walked in and said "Good, Mark you are here."

Mark laughed and replied, "Could I have dared to be late?"

"I am hungry. Can we go to the Coffee shop and have Mom's favorite burger with Fries?" asked Junior.

Brian asked him "Did you record next episode for your 'Love' presentation?"

Junior laughed and said "Yes, I did and that is why I am so hungry. Let us go."

Mark said "Okay, let us go but I am here to hear all you had to say about 'Why Love'."

They started walking towards the elevator. Junior grinned and said "Actually I should have consulted you and Brian first about it. You both loved Mom, didn't you?"

Mark softly murmured "Still do."

X X X

Junior had finished his first burger and was on his second one when Brian said "Okay you have had enough for now. Tell us about your presentation."

Junior kept munching Fries for some time. Then he said "Hmm, I only hope what I talked about would make some sense to the audience."

"Yes, it would! Never doubt son." Mark added softly.

Junior looked at them and began "Once I had asked Dad if it was true that to be happy, a man had to know that he was God. Dad had confirmed it. Do you know why? Because to become God, to feel like God, you must raise your vibration to the frequency of love. That is the most important reason why you need to learn to feel love. To be happy and satisfied in this virtual reality game, fall in love with life, fall in love with the game of life that we gods are playing.

Junior grinned at them and continued "To cut the long story short, Dad encouraged people to raise their vibration to the frequency of love, which is the frequency of their True Self, to make it possible for them to create a world of their dreams and live a happy life in this 3D physical world. Do I make sense?"

Mark nodded and Junior continued "The point to note here is the word 'RAISE', raise to the frequency of love. When you vibrate at a higher frequency, besides becoming powerful creators, your perception of the world changes, everything appears quite different as if you are seeing it through a lens of compassion/kindness/gratitude, all shades of love. When you vibrate at the frequency of love you are incapable of hurting anybody/anything. Your consciousness is different. You lead from your heart."

Junior looked at Brian and Mark with a smile. After a short pause he continued "Let me tell you something that I never told you, something that I experienced myself."

He said, "I knew Dad was not going to remain in this physical world for long."

Brian and Mark both were surprised and asked "What? How did you know?"

Junior replied "Hmm, I am not sure how I knew it but somehow, I did and so I tried to learn everything from Dad as soon as possible. I copied him so that when he was not here, I could take care of Mom as he used to do. Oh, how I copied and practiced! But when the time came Mom chose to leave with Dad! She didn't stay with me, for me! Oh, it hurt so much! I hurt, hurt, and hurt!"

Mark immediately said "No, you got it wrong son. You were Alaska's blue-eyed-boy. You don't know how much she loved you, Junior."

Brian added "You have indeed got it wrong because I know both Maxim and Alaska loved you intensely. They literally forced us to promise to take care of you in case they passed away from the physical reality before you were grown up."

"Yes, I know now. But that day I felt as if my heart was ripped apart. And then suddenly I felt the hum of high vibration in the hall. You do remember, don't you Brian, Mark? Everything hummed and vibrated till something popped open within me and I felt I was wrapped in love as never before. That day my parents changed my perception of the physical reality, by raising my vibration. This physical reality is not real. It is an illusion. We are playing a game for fun, for enjoyment, for new experiences.

I heard Dad saying 'We are just a thought away son. Think of us and you would immediately feel surrounded with love.'."

There was silence for a minute. Waiter came to serve more coffee to them.

Junior said with a smile "You see Mark, we must be able to raise our vibration to the frequency of love, that is the frequency of our True Self, while in this physical form, to change our perception of the world, of life itself and be free from self-inflicted sufferings."

Mark replied "Yes Junior, I understand it now. Thanks to you."

And Brian added "And I know, somehow, I must feel good, as much as possible, no matter what because by feeling good I maintain a higher frequency. Correct Junior?"

Junior laughed and replied "Yes, that is correct! After all we are here to enjoy the game of gods!"

CHAPTER 7

How To Use The Power Of 'Love': Generate Love

"WELCOME TO THE next presentation by Maxim de Winter jr." was written on the screen of the spiritual school. After a few seconds the camera caught sight of Junior running, skipping, jumping through a garden shouting "Hey Manda, wait, let me put on my jacket!"

"You are already on camera" came the answer.

"What? Oh alright. Sorry for being late." Then he waved his hands and asked "So what are we going to talk about today? Oh yes 'love'. It always is love, isn't it? Because love is the real reality. So, how to use the power of love to effortlessly create the life of your dreams and free you from sufferings."

Junior paused for a few seconds and then continued with his usual grin "Before we begin to discuss how to use the power of love you need to know how it feels. And before you feel it you need to know how to generate the energy that might make you feel the emotion of love."

He continued "Normally people think that the emotion one feels is dependent on outer circumstances but that is not always true. You can create feelings and emotions by thought alone! You must practice changing your thoughts on purpose, to see how it changes your emotions.

Anyways, you need to have thoughts, of or about, 'love' to generate the feeling of love. My mother, Alaska de Winter, declared it was easy, to begin with, by falling in love with yourself. She used to say you cannot love anything/anybody unless your own heart was overflowing with love.

So, to generate the energy of the required frequency of love, you may choose to fall in love with yourself. Yes, it does sound ridiculous even silly and selfish, but it is the short cut to the high vibration you need for the greatest good of all.

So, begin by changing your behavior. Treat yourself as you would treat a person you loved. You see, to raise your vibration you must feel love. Your vibration cannot be raised just by your saying that you love yourself. You must feel the emotion for it to be effective.

Should you find it difficult to grasp the unseen feeling of love, then I suggest you begin with romancing yourself. Why romance? What is the difference between love and romance? Well love is that unexplainable, that unreasonable deep liking for someone, for whom you could go to any lengths to care for, while romance is something new in your life, something exciting like flirting or the thrill of anticipating falling in love. Romance, to begin with, could be more fun, don't you think so? Romance may lead to love but not always. So, there is no tension, no pressure just fun and usually it does not touch your heart as deeply as love.

So, I repeat, to begin with, you practice romancing yourself. Feel the excitement, the thrill, the fun, the joy of romance and memorize the feeling. Rehearse it so that you can reproduce the feeling when you need it.

Other obvious way to learn to feel 'love', is to consciously desire to connect with your True Self, your 'I AM", because it vibrates at the frequency of love. So, how can you do it? Be curious. Ask 'Who am I'? Be persistent. Slow your breath. As your inhalation/exhalation slows down, so will your thoughts! If you keep practicing, a time will come when your thoughts stop for a couple of seconds and you will be left with an uncommon feeling of bliss, a kind of combined effect of love, joy, and peace, for no reason whatsoever! Well, you will feel this bliss only when you have reached or raised your vibration to the frequency of your True self, which is the frequency of love!

Junior paused. He dragged his fingers through his hair and waited for a few seconds. Then with a grin he started speaking "So far, I have talked how to raise your vibration to the frequency of love because 'love' is your main quest here. But first you must generate the energy, right? So, how do you do that?

It is well known that whatever we focus our attention on, gets empowered. So, then you can empower your creative energy by focusing your attention on or around the base of your spine where your creative energy resides. Breathing slowly through this center will enhance and build the creative energy.

Next, to feel the emotion, you must open your heart center in the center of your chest. To do that, you breath slowly with your attention focused on your heart. As you keep inhaling slowly, you will feel your creative energy rising from base of spine to your heart and further up your spine.

If you are sensitive, you might get the feeling of an orgasm, without any physical action. People with an irresistible zest for life, use consciously or unconsciously, the same process to ignite their creative passion. Passion is not lust and you can only feel true passion for something that you love. Anyway, it is the same creative energy. You choose what you wish to use it for.

I think now you know how to build and enhance your energy, how to raise its vibration to the frequency of love and how to open your heart center to feel the elevated emotion of love.

So, next week we can discuss how to use this divine power of love and create the life of your dreams."

Junior waved his hand and with his usual big grin, said "See you soon!"

CHAPTER 8

Jemma–The Green Eyed One

B RIAN WALKED IN into the De Winter residence and asked Carlos who had opened the door "Where is Junior?"

"He is in his studio, Sir."

"And where is Mark?"

Just then Mark walked in and said with a smile "Mark is right here Brian. What brings you here? Anyway, you are in time to share our Lemon-ice-tea and sandwiches."

Mark looked at Carlos and asked him to send Junior for the snack.

"No, hold on. I want to speak with you first Mark." Brian said.

Mark replied "Alright. We can talk in the library. Come!"

When both were inside the room, Mark turned to look at Brian and waited for him to speak.

After a moment Brian said, "Did you know that Junior was invited to and was expected to join the Williamson's boating party today?"

Mark replied "Yes, but he didn't want to go. I understand he called and informed them that due to some urgent work he won't be able to join them. Why, what happened? Something went wrong?"

Brian replied "Don't you think it is unnatural for a twenty-year young boy to be totally immersed in researching/ experimenting with the non-physical realm, as he says, and transcending the physical present to be in higher dimensions! You know Mark what he talks about. Margaret Williamson knows he loves boating, so she had gathered a dozen youngsters to throw a party for him, but he didn't go! She was disappointed."

After a short pause he continued "Mark, do you think, as his guardians, we are not doing our duty? Shouldn't we nudge him to play more with boys and girls of his age?"

Mark thoughtfully replied "Junior has a strong character. He is always bubbling with energy. He is loving and always ready to help anyone in need, but you cannot sway him from his chosen path. Hmmm but there is no harm in suggesting it to him. Let me call him for snack and we will see what we can do about it."

Before Mark could call Junior, he suddenly appeared in front of them with his usual grin and asked "What were you talking about? Am I in trouble?"

He looked at the table and said "Hey Mark I am hungry. Where are the sandwiches? Oh, there is Carlos with the food. Good".

Mark looked indulgently at Junior piling up his plate and said, "Come Brian, let us have some tea and give time to the boy to fill his tummy before we have our talk."

After munching away several sandwiches Junior asked "What is it you want to talk to me about, Mark? Brian?"

Mark said with a smile "Brian here thinks we have not been doing our duty as your guardian."

Junior said "What?" and burst out laughing.

Brian said "Today you were expected at Margaret Williamson's party. Why didn't you go Junior?"

Junior swallowed the sandwich and replied "Oh, it is about that, is it? Well, I had a lot of things to do here, much more interesting things, I may add. And Brian, I did telephone to inform them that I won't be able to join them. Thank you very much!"

Brian asked "Yes, I know, but my question was 'Why', why don't you find it interesting partying with boys and girls of your age? Usually people do, you know! Margaret is a very intelligent girl and beautiful too. She keeps inviting you, but you always find some excuse or the other, not to go. Why? All work and no play are not healthy."

Junior kept quiet for some time and then replied "Margaret is a nice girl, I agree Brian, but, somehow, spending time with her or her friends do not interest me. Sorry, maybe I am a misfit there. May be, due to my high frequency, my perception of the reality is quite different from theirs. I don't know Brian. Sorry.

Brian looked at Junior and said gently "I understand Junior, but you can surely adjust to others frequency level. Your father did it. Didn't he teach your mother to change her frequency as well, to match his, so as not to get shocked when he touched her? So, I suggest do try to mix with younger lot and have fun instead of working all the time. Who knows, you may meet someone like Alaska, as Maxim did, and fall in love with her?"

Junior looked incredulous for a moment. Then he asked "Hey Brian, I cannot believe it. Do you still think Dad met Mom by chance and fell in love with her? Dad's purpose for this incarnation was to find and live in this physical reality with Mom, his beloved Princess!"

Brian said with a sigh "Yes, I know. There was something special between them. Everyone could feel it. But Junior you are not carrying such an attachment from your past........"

Junior jumped in with "But Brian I am, and I have! Dad and Mom knew about my green eyed one. I told them about her when we went to Scotland last."

Junior closed his brilliant indigo eyes for a moment and murmured "I can still hear her last words 'Oh, Blue, my love!' I couldn't save her in that life but now I will. That is my promise!"

There was complete silence in the room for a short while.

Then Mark broke it and asked "I sensed there was someone but didn't want to ask you. Would you like to share your friend with us, yes, the green eyed one?"

Junior remained silent lost in his thoughts for some time. Mark thought Junior was not going to say anything, then he started speaking "I clearly remember the first time I saw her. I was trying to ride a new horse that my father, the laird, had got it that morning. As usual with a new horse, it was bucking and doing its best to throw me off and well, finally it did succeed. As I slipped off from the back of the horse, I heard the girl laugh loudly. I looked around but couldn't see her. The two stable boys who were with me, pointed towards a tree and I saw the girl with black hair and green eyes, full of life, laughing her head off. I glared at her and was just going to say something crushing to this annoying girl, when she surprised me.

She easily slid down from the branch of the tree and shook the dust from her skirt. And then she calmly started walking toward the rebelling horse with her arms stretched out in front. She kept murmuring something which I couldn't understand but I was surprised to see the horse calm down and let the girl wrap her arms around its neck! I was stunned. She patted the horse gently and continued talking with it for a few more minutes and then turned toward me and had said softly "You see your horse needs love. Never use brute force to control it."

Saying that she dipped in a semi curtsey and swiftly walked down the hill to the village I could see down below.

I didn't see her for a week or so. One day when I was returning from a visit to a neighboring laird, I saw her trying to reach for the flowers or fruits or something from a tree on a hillock. It was a bit high for her, so she kept jumping to reach it.

I went there and said "It seems your love is not good enough for the tree to bend down to you. Let me use my brute force and help you fill your basket with…..er..I don't see any fruit. What are you collecting?"

She turned around and had said "Oh, isn't it the laird offering to help me?"

I automatically corrected her "I am not the laird, my father is!"

She laughed. Her green eyes were shining in the setting sun. She had said "Yes, of course everyone knows you are not, but soon you will be!"

She stood there just staring at me and then suddenly she had said "God, have mercy on us! He is a real True Blue! I can see through his eyes!"

That somehow annoyed me. I asked her "What are you talking about?

She laughed and had said "Oh Blue, open your eyes and look at me, look at me. What do you see?"

She had opened her green eyes wide like saucers. I snapped, "What do you expect me to see?"

She laughed and had said "I see you are as dumb as that cow grazing in the field. Well, Blue, you are very much in need of some training. If you ask me nicely, I will teach you."

"Oh, really? Who do you think you are? You will teach me, will you? Do you even know how to read and write, foolish girl!" The moment those words came out of my mouth I regretted them.

I said "Sorry. That was rude. I didn't mean it."

The girl remained silent for a moment and then had said, "Forgive me my lord but the truth is I can tell you about things that you cannot sense with your five senses. But believe me they do exist. My father is a healer. I help him in his work. I collect the leaves, berries and herbs to make medicine to heal people with all kinds of diseases. Yes, I know you are the future laird. Yes, I know you have had best tutors to teach you, you have been to best schools and universities in the world, yet you cannot perceive the unseen realm right under your nose. You cannot read a man's silent thought. Won't you like to do that my lord?"

I kept staring at her brilliant green eyes, which, for once were bereft of all laughter. I was trying to decide if she meant what she said or if she was trying to make a fool of me.

She had surprised me by saying softly "No, I am not making fun of you. I will show you how to do it."

I was still not sure whether to believe her not, so I remained silent. After a few seconds she smiled. Her two dimples showed up on her cheeks which I had not noticed. I realized that she was a very beautiful girl.

She had said "I can read you Blue. You are wondering if I will really teach you anything, and if yes, then why do I want to teach you. Well, because you are the future laird, and you are intelligent and, I like you!" Saying this she picked up her basket and ran down the narrow path to the village.

Junior was silent, lost in his thoughts, for a little while. Then he continued "Next, I met her while returning from another neighboring clan helping them round up their sheep. I had somehow managed to have a big cut on my left wrist which was still bleeding.

I was in no mood to talk with her, but she had stopped me and had said "You are hurt Blue. Show me."

She took hold of my hand and unwrapped the scarf I had tied over the cut.

She had ordered "Close your eyes and repeat after me–'my wrists are healthy and strong'.

I don't know for how many times or for how long I repeated it. I came to the present when she had said "Open your eyes. Your wrist is back to normal."

Brian, I was stunned when I saw my wrist. Where was the wound, where was the bleeding cut? There wasn't even a scar! I looked at her in amazement.

I had asked her "What did you do?"

She had replied "I didn't do anything. You did it Blue. Didn't you say-'my wrist is healthy and strong? The omnipresent divine field had to obey your command, and so your wrist is normal as it is supposed to be!"

She smiled and had continued "Our Creator loves us, you see Blue, and is ever ready to do our bidding but because we cannot sense its presence with our five senses, we don't believe it."

I couldn't stop myself. I had to ask, "Do you sense this unseen Creator Jemma?" My stable boy had told me her name.

"Yes, I do and with practice, you too will. But today I need your help, or rather your father's, the laird's help." She had replied.

I asked "Why? What happened?"

She had explained "You know, we, I and my father, heal people in ways that they do not understand, but because they get healed, they come to father for treatment. Jack, the local blacksmith has been pestering my father to let him marry me. Last night when papa again refused him, he threatened to tell the villagers that I was a witch and so, I must be burned to keep the village and its people safe. Father has decided to leave the village tomorrow. He said there is only one person who could have helped us, that is, the laird, but he doesn't know us, so only solution is to leave the village."

I interrupted her "Father is not at home, but he will be back tonight. I will talk to him then. Ask your father to come and meet him tomorrow morning. Don't worry, you and your father are safe here. Jemma, I will keep you safe. Trust me."

Junior was silent for some time, still looking at the green lawn beyond the window. Then he resumed "The sun had set. It was turning dark. I was waiting impatiently for father to return. Just then Johnny, the stable boy, came in and told me that a little lad had come from the village and was begging to see me urgently.

I had a premonition. I ran out. The little lad was panting and crying at the same time. He could hardly speak but I understood. Some people had come to the village to kill Jemma and her father. I must come and save them.

I got on my horse and charged down to the village. I didn't plan, I didn't think of taking my guards. I had only one thought in my head–Jemma! I must save Jemma.

It was already dark but before I reached the village square, I saw a group of people standing around the pole with a fire lit at the base. Someone was tied to the pole. I knew it was Jemma.

I roared "Stop it!"

Jemma looked up and had screamed "Go back Blue! Get your guards!"

I heard her but how could I leave her. I was so angry I rode over to the center of the square and jumped down my horse to free her first, but it was not to be. My back was pierced with dozens of arrows and as I fell, I had heard her say 'Oh Blue, my love!"

Mark said softly "Oh my God."

Junior looked at Mark and Brian and asked, "Can you guess what happened next?"

Brian shook his head and said "No."

Junior continued "When the laird returned and came to know his beloved son was killed with a dozen arrows in his back, his grief and wrath knew no bounds. There was no mercy left in his heart. He ordered the village burned, everyone massacred!"

No one spoke for a minute.

Then Mark said, "I didn't know about your Jemma, my son, but I sensed your attachment to Scotland."

Brian asked "You said Your father incarnated only to live with his Princess, as he called Alaska, in this physical reality. So Junior, are you planning to do the same? Find Jemma in this 3D reality? Can you do it?"

"Yes, I can, and I shall! Dad said I will need unwavering patience with undiminishing desire. I am cultivating patience; you might have observed Brian." Junior said with a gentle smile.

CHAPTER 9

How to Use the Power of Love

SUN WAS JUST rising out of the ocean. Junior was standing with his arms wide open as if getting ready to embrace the mighty sun to his heart.

After waiting for a few minutes, the camera man said "I hope you are not planning to teleport somewhere Junior. We are here to telecast and record your talk on love, remember?"

Junior turned round to the camera and replied with a big grin "Roscoe, of course I remember. Shall we go inside for the recording? But I like it here. Will the sound of the waves and the wind distort the recording?"

"Go on, I can manage it Junior. Did I tell you; you already are on air?"

"Hey Roscoe, you always do that! You enjoy doing that, don't you?" laughed Junior and waved his hands and said "So, today we talk about love, as usual. You know how to generate energy and create the feeling of love whenever you want to. That is what we did last week.

Today we will see how to use this power of love to easily and effortlessly create the life of your dreams.

You know Gladiator's formula for manifesting your desires like an ultimate magician, literally out of thin air without lifting a finger.

The formula is–
1. Dream
2. Follow your dream.
3. Live the life of your dream.

He always used the word 'dream'. So, what is the difference between a desire and a dream? Well, he explained, a desire you love turns into a dream. An ordinary desire gets elevated to the position of dream only when you love it. As you know, you cannot be passionate about a desire that you do not love. You need to ignite your creative passion for your desire/goal/vision/mission to bring it to life in this physical reality effortlessly. To give life to anything you must love it.

So then, use the power of love to upgrade your ordinary desire to a dream, a dream, just the thought of which, makes you excited and thrilled, and that skyrockets your frequency. This is the first step.

The second step is: Follow your dream. As you love your desire it will be natural for you to feel good, feel happy and maintain a high vibration while visualizing, imagining your dream life, even before it is in your 3D physical reality. You will not be troubled by negative thoughts and doubts because you would be vibrating at the high frequency of love.

I think, now you can see the obvious benefits of learning to love and to feel it in your heart, in other words, to raise your vibration to the frequency of love and remain anchored in it.

Alright, the third step: Live the life of your dreams. Well, in perfect divine time, Quantum Field will manifest your dream world. Enjoy it. Inspire others to create and live their dream lives."

Junior paused and looked around, then continued with his usual grin "Yes, you can very well ask what about an ordinary desire, a desire that you do not really love or feel for? What happens to those desires? Can't you manifest them?

You see, a dream that makes you come alive, is generally your life's true purpose. Once you achieve it, your other little desires will automatically fall into place without any struggle on your part. Your joy of achieving your true purpose, its high frequency will ensure your little desires get fulfilled just by desiring them!

But should you have another little desire that you wish to fulfill, you can do it by whipping up your desire, by changing your thoughts about it. As you change your thoughts, your feeling, your emotion would change about your little desire. It would not remain your 'little' desire anymore. It would have become a desire that you love, a dream. A touch of love is all that is needed to manifest your goals/desires!

You must practice getting the knack of feeling 'love,' if you do not already have it. The magic is in feeling love. It is not available in the open market, but you can have it for free, if you wish to. It is your choice.

So, go ahead, enjoy this feeling of unconditional love for FREE!"

Junior waved his hand and said, "See you next week!"

CHAPTER 10

Creator or Victim

JUNIOR STOOD ON the deck and looked at the open space behind the house.

"Master, dinner is served. Mr. Mark is waiting for you." Said Carlos.

Junior turned and said with a laugh "Hey Carlos, do I look like a master? Dad is the master."

"Mr. Brian says we must address you as master but if you like I can call you the Young Master." Carlos replied with a grin.

Junior laughed and went in to join Mark.

Mark looked up at Junior and said "Come, cook has made something special for you."

"Oh." Junior didn't say anything after that.

"You seem to be lost somewhere. What is it Junior? Can I help?" asked Mark.

Junior looked up from his plate and said "Yes, Mark, you can help me."

Mark waited for Junior to speak. After swallowing couple spoonful of food, he said "You know today I had my weekly presentation recorded for the spiritual school. I had to tell them the benefits of touching their thoughts with love. So, to start with I reminded them of Dad's formula–Dream, follow your dream and then live the life of your dreams.

Mark, a thought has been nagging me since then. Dad, or rather Gladiator, had already explained it to them but they didn't get it! Why? Because they don't want to understand it, or because they have made their choice to feel like victims of their life's circumstances, instead of the creators? Do they enjoy being victims? Anyways then, is there any use my trying to explain it to them? Tell me Mark, tell me, should I continue with my presentations?"

Mark said with his gentle smile "You must continue Junior, you must! Thousands of people got it from Gladiator. I am one of them. Your mother was another! Our consciousness is changing, slowly but surely. A lot of people are now aware of their 'Awareness,' the non-physical, boundless, multi-dimensional being that we truly are. A lot of people know that we are not this physical being, that physicality is an illusion. So, yes, you must continue telling them what you learned from your parents. Another thousand will get it from you and so it will go on. One day humanity will know that they are not only physical humans but non-physical formless divine too!"

Junior's indigo eyes were shining when he said "Oh Mark, you are so right! Okay, so I must tell them and make them believe that they are the creators of their, so called physical reality, and that they should create, of course, with love, like an ultimate magician, without moving a finger, literally out of thin air! Right Mark?"

"Right son! That is what your parents said. I trust them."

CHAPTER 11

How to Use the Power of Love: Highs and Lows

"**H**EY, THE ULTIMATE magicians of Gladiator, I trust you have rehearsed the feeling, the emotion of love, and/or all shades of love, sooooo.. many times, that you can reproduce it whenever you wish it" said Junior while running down the steps.

As soon as he reached the level ground in the garden, he continued with his usual grin "The challenge you face is to differentiate between thinking and feeling. Usually when you believe you are feeling you are still in your head. You must move out of your head and be down in your heart to feel the elevated emotion of love, and/or shades of love, like compassion, kindness, gratitude, joy, peace, freedom and anything else that makes you feel good.

The breeze had picked up. His hair was all over his forehead and his indigo eyes were twinkling like stars. With a laugh he said "Alright, let us begin. So, you are happy, excited, your creative juices bubbling and you know your dream is on its way. You don't have any limiting or contrary beliefs to sabotage the manifestation. Sounds great, doesn't it? Well, this is the period of 'High', you feel you are on top of the world. Why? Because you are vibrating at a high frequency, like the frequency of love, or joy or the frequency of your True Self. It is one and the same. No one, nothing in this physical world can make you truly happy if you are not vibrating at a high frequency. At best, the joy you could expect from a thing out there, can only be fleeting."

Junior paused, ran his fingers through his hair and continued with a grin "Okay, that was a description of you being on a 'High', in other words, you were vibrating at the high frequency of love or shades of it.

Now let us see what happens when you vibrate at a lower, denser frequency like fear, and/or shades of fear, like anger, frustration, envy, jealousy, conflict and anything else that makes you feel bad. You don't feel good, you hate it, everything annoys you, you are full of thoughts of revenge, you feel a failure, a victim etc.! Now you are in 'Lows' because you have allowed your vibration to plunge down to the low frequency of fear. No one, nothing in this world can make you feel happy because you are vibrating at the low frequency. You know when you feel fear it is a clear indication you are out of alignment with your True Self. Your True self is telling you it does not agree with your views, feelings or action on the subject. You must change your thoughts, feelings to align with the divine guidance of your True Self. You also lose the magical power of love the moment your thoughts are based on fear and its likes."

Junior stopped for a few seconds, then asked "What do I mean by the magical power of love? Well, when your thoughts are fear based you cannot create like an ultimate magician anything out of nothing. You lose the power to create your dream, your goal effortlessly, if you are not vibrating at the high frequency of your True Self, which is love."

Junior paused and looked at the screen expectantly, as if waiting to get some answer, and may be, he got the silent response from his unseen audience because he continued "So, when you find yourself in a grip of some negative thoughts, and emotions, what should you do? How do you get out of it? How do you change it and feel good again? Please do not try to push it out of your life or push it under the carpet or try to ignore it or forget it or keep blaming others for years to come. Please don't! If you do so, your negative thoughts will be attracting more of the same in your life and the negative energy of the thoughts will get lodged in your physical body to show up later as disease.

You know you are the creator of your physical reality (which is not really real). Anyway, all you perceive is created by you, starting by your thought and imagination. But why, why did you create something that you judge as bad? Can you guess? It got created, I think, because you needed to experience it, before you could evolve to higher dimension! In any case, it is there to help you, so you should embrace the experience with all gratitude you can manage to feel in your heart. Can you accept it with love, as a gift from your True Self? That is the right attitude to have, not to resist it but to embrace it! You see our Creator never excludes anything. It embraces everything and keeps expanding.

To begin with, not to resist but to embrace the painful circumstance, will not be easy for your ego. Your analytical mind, the little 'i' as I call it, will resist it tooth and nail! It will give you hundreds of reasons why you must crush it, throw it out of your life.

But now you do know, don't you, why you will not allow yourself to do that. The more you think of getting rid of the unpleasant thing/circumstance the more your thought will remain focused on it. The more your thought remains focused on it the Field will deliver more of the same to you. This is the loop of thinking and creating. You may love the thought, or you may dread the thought, it will have no effect on the result. What you think, will get created, and once it is created, follow the golden rule, that is, embrace it with gratitude!"

Junior continued with a smile, "Now you have seen the power of love in action, both in manifesting your dream and in getting free from unwanted manifestation! 'Love' is the answer for all!

Junior's indigo eyes were twinkling when he asked "Does it make sense? It will, once you start to practice it in your daily life. Alright, next comes Dominant energy under the heading 'How to use the power of love'. Shall we keep this discussion for next week? Yes?"

He laughed and waved his hand and said, "See you soon."

CHAPTER 12

Power of Belief

MARK SMILED WHEN he heard Junior running up the steps two at a time and yelling "Hey Mark where are you? I am hungry. Has Brian come?"

Mark came out of the study and said "Come and eat. No, Brian has not arrived yet. Should be coming now. What is the hurry?"

Junior replied with a huge grin "See, I got a bottle of Crystal water for Brian. It will help him relax and feel better."

Mark asked "Will it, really? Junior if your answer is 'yes' then let the De Winter Enterprises bottle and sell it. You will be doing a great service to humanity."

Junior replied, "My answer is 'yes', but as you know, people would not believe it."

Mark continued with his questions "Do you mean if they do not believe in its therapeutic powers, it won't help/ heal them?"

Junior looked surprised and said "Mark, you know it. You know the unimaginable power of belief in creation. Dad used to say, 'anything is possible if you can believe it'.

Remember? But the flip side is also true. Nothing is possible if you do not believe it!"

Mark murmured "The placebo and the nocebo effect."

Junior said "Yes. The medicine helps because the sick person believes in the goodness of the medicine, and he also believes in the brilliance of the doctor who prescribed it. In truth, it is his belief that heals his body. A non-belief can sabotage your best laid plan in any area of your life."

Mark asked "Junior, can one change one's belief then?"

Junior smiled and said "Yes, but one has to be aware of his negative and/or contrary beliefs."

"Ah, therein lies the rub, doesn't it? Anyways, do tell me some simple ways to change my detrimental beliefs, son." Said Mark.

"Mmm Mark, you radiate peace. Any detrimental belief, if you had one, would have dissolved in it." Junior said.

"But, if you want to know, let me tell you how to change one's belief. Well, once you are aware of the limiting belief, easiest way to convince your analytical mind to let it go, would be to point out the reason why you wish to do so. You cannot fight your belief and win it, but a logical explanation or a scientific proof against it will shake the root of your old belief. It may take time, but I think it is the right way to go about changing your limiting beliefs. Of course, there are many other ways you can choose from, to get free of your negative beliefs. You may like to use the guided meditation, hypnotherapy, E.F.T., past life regression therapy etc.," said Junior.

Just then Brian walked in the room. He asked "What is going on? Who needs a therapy?"

Junior said "I don't think anyone needs a therapy here, but do you, Brian? No, you need rest not therapy. I prepared a bottle of crystal water for you. You remember Dad used to make crystal water? They are very effective. This water is fully charged with peace vibration. Yes, I played the piano for half an hour with the water and the crystal in front of me. I know the water has absorbed the peace vibration. Drink it every morning. You will feel rejuvenated and at peace Brian. Will you do it for me?"

"I will do anything for you Junior, you know it. Thank you. I am grateful." Said Brian emotionally.

"Ah, therein lies the rub, as Mark would say. Don't drink it because I asked you to. Drink it because of its healing power, the rejuvenating power that I induced the water with, by playing your favorite music. Believe it when you sip the water every morning. Will you Brian? Not for me but for yourself?" asked Junior with his usual grin.

By now Brian and Mark were laughing.

Brian said "You remind me of Alaska so much. You must get your way, somehow or the other? Right Junior? Anyway, I like you vey much, you bundle of mischief and magic! Yes, I will sip this water, this ordinary water believing it to be a magical potion that would transform me. Happy?"

Junior replied with a laugh "In a month I will know if you drank the water with the belief in its powers or not. I will catch you, Brian!"

Mark said with a smile, "Alright son, time to eat."

Brian laughed and said, "Yes Junior, after all you are the master magician. Right?"

"Right, Brian!" laughed Junior.

CHAPTER 13

How to Use the Power of Love: Beware of Thoughts That Lower Your Vibration

"JUNIOR, MAKE YOURSELF visible! You are on! Come on now!" muttered the camera man at the spiritual school.

And then, suddenly out of nowhere we see the dashing young man, Mr. Maxim de Winter jr., standing in front laughing his head off!

The camera man, with a reluctant smile asked "Could you enlighten us a little? How and why, you make yourself invisible when I am recording you?"

With an ear-to-ear grin Junior replied "Yes, of course! I think it will make people curious. People may want to learn to make themselves visible and invisible as and when they wish to. It is easy. You become invisible to human eye by raising your frequency to such an extent that you move to a higher dimension."

"And where is this higher dimension, may one ask?" he asked.

"Why, it is right here! Only human eye cannot see it." Junior replied with a grin.

He looked around for a few seconds and then began "Alright, let us begin. So, you know you must maintain a high frequency dominant energy if you wish to create or manifest your vision out of thin air or otherwise. You must be awake to, or conscious of, your dominant feelings. It needs diligence, a lot of diligence on your part, but it is fun at the same time to keep a check on your feelings/emotions. If you wish to avoid feeling disappointed or like a failure, you need to maintain a joyful dominant vibration all the time, which means, vibrate at the frequency of 'love' or shades thereof."

Junior stopped, ran his fingers through his hair and then continued "Let me give some examples. There are three main areas in your life that inadvertently aids in lowering your vibrations if you are not careful. Beware of them. First is, the story you tell yourself about yourself. Does the story make you feel empowered, successful, or weak, like a victim? If it is the later, you must change it."

"Allow me to tell you about a girl who had written her first book and was being interviewed by a publisher. She was very nervous.

Publisher said,-"Pitch yourself."

Girl said-"What?"

Publisher-"I understand you are an author. What do you write about?"

Girl-"Spiritual fiction."

Publisher smiled and said in a dismissing way-"Oh, fiction!"

Publisher's attitude made her hackles rise.

Girl-"I am publishing my book under the genre of Spiritual Fiction but in truth it is a Self-help book."

Publisher-"Really? What do you want the world to know from this Self-help book of yours?"

Girl-"We are the creators of our physical reality. We never were or will ever be a victim of circumstances or anything else. I want everyone to know this and go right ahead creating the life of their dreams."

Publisher-"Why should anyone care?"

Girl-"Everyone should and will care about it. Humanity is suffering. People are drowning in pessimism and feel helpless, discouraged. A new way of life is needed now."

Publisher-"And you think your book will usher in a new way of life?"

Girl said boldly,-"Yes!"

The interview carried on for some time, but it made the girl change her story she had been telling herself. She used to think she and her book were at the mercy of the publisher and the readers. Will they like it, will they publish it, she had worried. In other words, subconsciously she thought and felt like a victim! The most disempowering thought! With this pitching interview she got the clarity, and she changed her story. The new narrative made her a powerful creator/author instead of a meek victim of the publisher and the readers.

Usually, when you feel stuck in a rut, the culprit is the story you tell and believe about yourself."

Junior continued "The second area you should watch is your reaction to your family-your spouse, your parents, your siblings, your children. Do any of them always irritate you, push your button, so to speak? If so, you must change your reaction to them. Remember, your outer world is the reflection of your inner world. All your family members are simply reflecting you, the inner you. They are in your life to help you get beyond your usual reaction of irritation. Next time when someone annoys you, say with a smile 'thank you for helping me' silently or aloud as per your preference. The change in them will surprise you, believe me, and some of those people may even move out of your life, once you change yourself. Never react to your family in a way that lowers your vibration."

Junior paused for a few seconds and then said "Third area. Most common. Do you find yourself blaming others for all ills in your life? Blame the government, blame the city, blame the office, blame the traffic, blame the weather, blame the doctor, the medicine, lack of time, lack of money...... anything and everything, blame it on others! I don't know if blaming makes you feel any better, but one thing is for sure-it will lower your vibration considerably, which you cannot allow. You are the creator. If you created something that you do not like, then change it, don't blame it on others."

Junior turned to look at someone and asked, "Hey Joss, it was you who told me about a 'smart Aleck' who was quick to find faults, wasn't it you?"

He got his answer "Yes, it was me."

Junior laughed and continued "Well, you may enjoy being called a smart Aleck but finding faults is not a good idea. Why? Because when you think or focus on faults, yours or others, you again lower your vibration."

Junior said with a big grin "Watch out for thoughts that may bring down your vibration! After all vibrating at the high frequency of love or shades of love, is prerequisite for manifesting your desire out of thin air!"

Of course, there are other ways to maintain an elevated emotion. We will talk about it later."

Junior waved his hands with a slow dazzling smile that reminded everyone of his mother, Alaska de Winter and said "So long. Will see you soon."

CHAPTER 14

Our Universe is Abundant

B RIAN PEEPED IN and asked "Junior, do you have a moment free?"

Junior looked surprised and asked with a grin "Why? I was only going to the spiritual school, but I always have a moment to spare to listen to my guardian's lecture! What is it, Brian?"

Brian said, "We have just finished Board of Director's meeting and they would like to meet you, Junior. They want to hear from you, how you keep the 'doorway to abundance' open for De Winter Enterprises without doing anything. Could you also explain to them, why you say, 'lack cannot exist in our universe'. Will you?"

With a twinkle in his indigo eyes, he said "But Brian I am hungry!"

Brian laughed and said "Yes, you are always hungry like Alaska. I know. I KNOW! Snacks and drinks are over there. Come now."

Junior entered the hall with Brian and greeted the Directors. He was met with genuine welcome from a dozen of well-dressed ladies and gentlemen. It was obvious everyone was very fond of him. They had seen him grow up from a little boy to his present age of twenty. This 6 ft. plus young man, with his indigo laughing eyes, reminded them of his charismatic father. He indeed had a magnetic personality. People found him irresistibly attractive which, as per Gladiator, was due to his high frequency of vibration. It had nothing to do with his good looks. As a matter of fact, he always seemed to be bubbling with joy and exuding a kind of magnetic energy waves that pulled everything towards him. On top of it, he had inherited his mother's infectious smile to boot.

Junior invited the Directors "Please come and do some justice to the sandwiches and the cakes spread on this table. They look delicious, don't they?"

Everyone agreed and joined him. For next 10 minutes or so people were busy eating and drinking.

Then one of the ladies asked Junior with a smile "If you have had enough to eat, could I ask you a question?"

Junior grinned and said "Please do. I can continue eating, if you don't mind?"

The lady laughed and asked "Tell us how do you keep the business, the money, the good-will for De Winter Enterprises growing day-in day-out? How do you keep the doorway to abundance, so to speak, open without doing anything?"

Junior looked surprised and stopped eating. He said, "I? I do nothing! De Winter Enterprises has given me so much joy, what could I do but love it? I love the people working with us in different departments, in different cities of the world. It has its own life. It will prosper and keep on expanding till the people working here like and love to work here! Yes, it is their love that keeps it going, that gives it its life."

There was silence in the room.

The lady asked "You really mean it? That is the truth behind its success?"

Junior smiled and replied "Yes, that is the truth. People's love for it, gives it its life. That is the secret of its success."

After a moment's silence someone asked, "Brian here tells us one of your favorite statements is 'Lack cannot exist'. Tell us, son, what do you mean by that."

Junior smiled and said "What I mean is exactly what it says Sir, that is, lack cannot exist. How can lack exist in our boundless, limitless, infinite universe? Idea of lack is a creation of our logical mind. It cannot be true, and I know for sure it is the most disempowering idea ever created."

Junior took a gulp of his iced tea and asked, "How do you explain 'lack'? Suppose I had a dollar and I decide to give it to you, then, I will be lacking the dollar. Is that it? Well, sir, our infinite universe does not work like that.

You see, our universe is made of energy, only energy. Physicality is an illusion. So, the dollar is also energy. When I give you my dollar, I am giving you energy. As per the universal law, the Quantum Field will rush to fill in the vacuum created by my giving you the dollar! So, I will get something in exchange for the dollar I gave you. So, you see, I would never lack anything, ever. The field will always compensate my generosity by replacing it and balancing it with some kind of energy. So, lack, is not possible in our universe. You give something, you get something in exchange. That is how energy circulates. In fact, when you give something, you start the energy moving. Yes, you begin circulation of energy. There is no lack involved in circulating energy., is there?"

Junior drank half a glass of water and continued with his usual grin "I think you will find it interesting to know, how the Quantum Field decides what I should get in exchange for my dollar. Quantum Field ensures no vacuum is left but how does it decide what to give? Well, the Field reads the frequency of my vibration at the time I gave my dollar. Was I worried at its loss, worried how will I buy my food? If I was unhappy, the Field will, of course, give me something in exchange, but somehow it won't give me joy. I will not be able to enjoy it. But suppose I gave the dollar lovingly, I will get something that will bring more love, more joy in my life. Simple, isn't it?"

Junior paused and looked at Brian "I am late Brian. Can I go now?"

Brian looked at the Directors and they said "Thank you Mr. De Winter. We appreciate your spiritual explanations. We hope to see you soon."

Junior replied with twinkling eyes "I hope so too. It is always a pleasure to meet with you."

Saying that, in a blink of an eye, he just vanished from the hall leaving the Directors stunned.

"Where did he go?" they asked.

Brian replied with a shake of his head "By now he must be at the school."

"He has supernatural powers like his father." They exclaimed.

Brian replied with a smile "He doesn't agree, just like his father. Maxim used to say 'we are born with these powers. It is natural to all of us.' "

"Really?" they asked.

"Please join the club, and join the Spiritual school. You will have the answer." Said Brian. They all laughed.

CHAPTER 15

How to Use the Power of Love: Kinds of Suffering

J UNIOR STOOD SILENTLY lost in thought.
Camera man gently prompted him "Mr.de Winter, say something. You are on!"
"What? Oh yes, I was thinking of different ways that the power of love could be used.

So, you know how to use the power of 'love' to manifest your desire effortlessly, and, also how to use it to let go with gratitude the thing you didn't want in your life.

Alright, today we talk about human suffering. What causes it. You do wish to be free of suffering, don't you? Most common causes of suffering are—First—you don't have what you want, and second—you have what you don't want in your life. As explained earlier, you know how to be free of these sufferings by consciously feeling love, gratitude and other shades of love.

Did you know there is another kind of suffering that humans face? Have you heard about artists, musicians, geniuses who have attained name, fame and success in their respective fields, and yet they are not happy. They get so depressed that a time comes when they want to end their lives! This happens to people who are disconnected with their True-Self. Nothing satisfies them. This is caused by the pain of separation from their True self. They are not aware of it, but their heart craves the unconditional love of the Creator.

Remedy for them is to connect with their True self. You already know your True self vibrates at the frequency of love, the unconditional love. In other words, it is love for no reason.

Now, your ego mind, the little 'i', that you are so proud of and rightly so, is analytical by nature. It never does anything without a reason. After all it is there to weigh the pros and cons before allowing you to proceed.

So then, to be able to connect with your True self, the big 'I', you must leave your mental abode in your head and literally descend to your heart in the center of your chest. With your attention focused on your heart, your energy will flow to the heart and open the center. As you breathe slowly in and out of your heart, your creative energy from the base of your spine might be pulled up with a sensation like an orgasm to your heart. When your heart opens like the petals of a flower, you experience the illusive big 'I', the unconditional love or the love for no reason, yes, that is your True self! You need a lot of practice, patience and an unwavering desire to know it. Do not try to understand it because it is beyond the comprehension of your analytical mind."

Junior paused, looked around and with a wide grin continued "Have you heard the story of a wave who wanted to know the ocean? Yes, that is right, the wave had to lose its identity and merge itself to know the ocean. Similarly, the little 'i', your analytical mind, must be ready to lose its identity of being the little 'i', and merge itself nto the big 'I', your True self, to know the True self (vibrating at the frequency of love)! Simply said, to know the True self one must become the True self.

So, for a man to be free from all kinds of suffering, to be truly happy, he needs to raise his vibration to the frequency of love, which is the frequency of his True self.

Junior said with a smile "That is enough for today. Next week we will talk about the little 'i', how it got its identity etc. Take care. See you soon."

CHAPTER 16

Could She Be My Green Eyed One?

J UNIOR ENTERED THE house at a run asking "Hey Mark, why were you looking for me? Everything okay?"

Mark came out of the living room and replied with a gentle smile "Yes, everything is okay. I want you to meet my young friend here. She is daughter of Julie. You remember Julie, Alaska's college friend?"

Junior took off his jacket and replied "Yes, of course I remember. She is the one who became a doctor."

Mark said "Yes, she is the one. She is a very successful doctor, thanks to your father. Anyway, Juliana, her daughter, is here on a school trip. Come Juliana, meet Maxim junior."

Junior looked at the girl who came forward and was stunned. She had the same Emerald green-eyes. Could she be his Jemma? Could she? Could she be his green eyed one? She had the same shiny black hair and green eyes, and she kept looking at him through those eyes without blinking even once!

Tense silence broke when she spoke in a hushed voice, "Oh my God! Is he Gladiator?"

That brought Junior back to the present. He murmured "Oh Dad, I am tired of competing with you."

Mark laughed and said "No, Juliana. He is not Gladiator. He is Maxim jr., Gladiator's son. Yes, he does resemble his father a lot."

Mark looked at Junior and said, "Did I forget to tell you Juliana and her mother are great fans of your father?"

Junior said "Huh!"

Juliana looked shocked at his reaction and said, "What do you mean by 'Huh'? You are privileged to look like Gladiator! My God, he was so handsome, so powerful, so so….attractive! Anything I ever ask he gets it done! What about you mister 'Huh', can you do anything?"

Junior was bereft of speech for a few seconds. Then he laughed and said "Miss Green eyes, you may be Dad's fan, but obviously he failed to teach you a thing. Such a pity!"

Juliana snapped "What do you mean, Mr. Blue eyes?"

Junior was still reeling at her appearance. He was still trying to ascertain if she could be his Jemma. Did she remember him, but the answer eluded him.

Mark was watching the interaction between the two with interest. Then, with a smile he said "Come on, Junior, Juliana is our guest. Stop baiting her."

Junior sighed and replied "I was not baiting her. She challenged me. She asked if I could do things that Dad could. Just imagine Mark, it was Dad who always pointed out to everyone that he was not a supernatural being. What he could do, anyone could do, because we were born with the same powers."

Juliana murmured "No, I was not challenging you, but I hate people who try to belittle his power. I love Gladiator, you see!"

Junior grinned and said "Yes, I see that. Despite my ongoing competition with him, believe me, I do admire him and love him. He is my father, you see!"

Juliana giggled at that and said "Yes, I see that. Junior, did you know your eyes are indigo blue, aren't they? You are a true blue. Can I call you True Blue?"

Junior was silent for a second. He couldn't reply. He remembered Jemma had once asked him same question.

Juliana felt awkward when he didn't answer. She quickly said "Sorry, please forgive......"

Junior immediately said "Of course you can. Nothing to forgive. You reminded me of a friend from my past who used to call me Blue."

Juliana asked "Really? Where does she live?"

Junior replied "I am not sure, but rest assured I will let you know when I find out. Okay, now I am going to teach you that you can be, do and have anything you wish for, if you can believe it."

Mark said "Good. Juliana, I have some work to do. I will be back in an hour to drive you back to your hotel."

Junior interrupted "I can drive her back Mark."

Mark smiled and said "Good. We will both drive her back. Alright Juliana?"

"Yes, Uncle Mark." She replied.

As Mark left them, Junior quizzed Juliana "Uncle?"

Juliana replied "Of course I call him uncle. He was my mother's college friend as well as your mothers. He is so gentle and understanding, I really like him."

Junior thought for a while, then said, "I am not sure why, but I have always thought him to be my friend. I was very possessive of him. I would never let him talk with Mom and Dad for long. It is quite funny because Mark usually calls me 'son', but I feel he is MY friend. And I more than like him. He and Brian have been my anchor in this 3D physical reality after my parents decided to exit it when I was barely fifteen. Er... I don't know why I am telling you all this....."

Juliana grinned and reached out for his hand and said "Be my friend, Blue! Will you?"

Junior grabbed her hands and replied gruffly "Okay, so you got a blue-eyed friend! Now, pay attention. I am going to teach you some basic spiritual truths so that you won't need to ask Dad to help you. You will be able to do the things yourself and teach it to your friends as well.

First, know that you are the creator of your so-called 3D reality. You could create like an ultimate magician out of thin air without lifting a finger, if you so wished.

So, how do you create? You create by your thoughts, beliefs, imagination, feeling and resulting emotion. Anything you can imagine you can create. You also need to believe in your inherent powers to create. Just saying it, is not enough. You must believe it.

Suppose you want a different life; you wish to have different circumstances. So then, what do you do? First, you ignore the current reality. You transcend the reality that you don't want in your life. Second, imagine and/or visualize the reality that you wish for, till you feel that you already have it in your life, before it is! Don't doubt the process. It will be delivered to you in perfect time. Trust it!

Begin by changing your thoughts. Your changed thoughts will change your feelings and emotions, and your changed feelings/emotions will change your physical reality. In other words, you change your thoughts, you change your physical reality.

Did you wonder how? You see our universe is energy. Our thoughts vibrate at certain frequencies. So, when you desire something, your thoughts vibrate at the frequency of your desire, and the Quantum Field which reads the frequency, will deliver your desire to you in perfect time. Does it make sense? Anyways this is how the creation works. I really don't know how much of spiritual laws you are acquainted with. You will have to ask me if anything is not clear to you."

Juliana smiled and nodded her head.

Junior said with a big grin "Now is the time for some magic to excite you, to awaken you." And the next moment he opened his hand to show a golden pen.

Juliana's eyes were round with surprise. She said "That is my pen. How did you get it?"

Junior threw back his head and laughed out loud. He said, "It is magic, little girl!"

Juliana implored "No. Tell me how did you do it? When did you take my pen? Tell me!"

"Okay, okay, listen" said Junior "I will go step by step. Tell me when I said 'you' create your reality. Who is that 'you' I talk about?"

Juliana looked confused. She asked "Who?"

Junior grinned and said "I asked you. You must answer. Alright I will help you. I give you two options to choose from. Are 'you' this physical body, Juliana, daughter of such and such or are you non-physical boundless Awareness, a consciousness, that is beyond space and time and is eternal. Think and answer."

Juliana thought and thought frowning and getting angry with herself for not being able to decide who this 'you' was.

Junior was whistling some tune while waiting for her answer. He was looking at her intensely and wondering if she was his green eyed one. He was getting impatient. Just then he remembered his father telling him 'You will need unwavering patience and undiminishing desire to find her' and he laughed and silently said 'thanks for reminding me Dad.'

He said "Come Juliana, don't be angry, I will tell you. You are non-physical being having a physical experience, or you can even say, you are playing a virtual reality game for fun. You are, and you have, boundless Awareness. You are multi-dimensional consciousness beyond space and time. You have this physical body, but you are not it, you are much more! You are powerful beyond the comprehension of your logical mind. Believe it! Once you believe it you will know for sure that you are the creator of your reality without any doubt."

Junior paused and then asked, "Did I bore you?"

Juliana jumped with "No, no, keep talking. I want to know the spiritual truths Blue. Don't stop. Please Blue, please!"

Junior said with a smile "Okay, then let me tell you how to connect and be aware of your real self, the non-physical Self, ever present, ever awake Self. It is easy. Follow me. Relax. Calm yourself. Nothing to worry, nothing to do except, breathe! Slowly inhale, slowly exhale, stop thinking for a couple of seconds! Don't be tense. Just keep your thoughts at bay for a few seconds."

After keeping silent for a minute Junior asked her "How did you feel? Or rather, what did you feel? Can you give it a name? Peace, expansion, freedom, joy–anything? I know, it is difficult to describe it, but when you stop your thoughts, what you are left with, is your Self, your True self."

Juliana looked confused. She said, "I don't know what I felt."

Junior laughed and said "That is okay. You need to practice it at home."

"No, please do it once more." She begged.

Junior looked at her indulgently and did it, not once but several times with her till she got the hang of it. Now that she could feel something she could not stop laughing.

Junior closed his eyes and listened to her infectious laughter. Finally, he asked "So, how do you feel Green eyes?"

"Happy! I feel happy Blue." She spoke.

Junior looked at her with approval in his indigo eyes and said "You got it! Our essential nature is happiness, happiness for no reason. Now practice it as often as you remember to."

"Yes, I will Blue!" she said still laughing.

Junior said with a grin "There are other ways to become aware of your True self. Most of these doorways to your True self are based on raising your vibration to the frequency of love or shades of love like joy, gratitude, compassion etc. "

"Love? Why love?" she asked.

"Because your, natural state of being is love!" grinned Junior.

Just then Mark walked in and looked at them. He said "Oh, I see, you two are still busy."

Junior said "We were but no more. It is enough for one day."

Juliana cried "Oh no, I need to ask you so many questions. You did not tell me how you got my pen Blue. And how I can be sure that I create my reality? And how……oh no, you must answer me before I let you go!"

Junior laughed and said "Now you are behaving exactly like the green-eyed witch I knew once! Listen, you need to digest the information I gave to you today otherwise you will get indigestion. Your body needs time to integrate it in its system. In the meantime, you contact our spiritual school. They will help you. We have got the best teachers. After a month or so, when you are ready for more, I will tell you more."

"How? I will be back in Boston!" she wailed.

Junior replied "Hey, don't cry. I don't like to see your green eyes swimming in tears! I will meet you when you are ready to learn more, may be, I will teleport to Boston! Who knows? Anything is possible if you can believe it Juliana!"

She asked "Are you kidding? Could you really come to Boston to teach me?"

Juliana turned towards Mark and asked him "Uncle Mark, do you think he means it? Will he come to Boston?"

Before Mark could respond to her question Junior said, "Trust me!"

Juliana kept staring into his indigo eyes for a long time and then nodded her head and said, "I will wait for you Blue!"

Mark was smiling but remained silent. He kept wondering if Juliana could be Junior's Jemma. Why did she call him Blue? Surprising! No one else ever called him Blue. Could this young girl be the one whose last words to Junior were 'oh, Blue my love'?

Junior nodded and said "Mark let us go and eat somewhere. I am hungry. After the meal we will drop Juliana at the hotel."

Mark said, "Come children, let us go and find something tasty to eat. For a change I am also hungry. What about you Juliana? Hungry?"

Juliana smiled and replied, "Yes uncle Mark, I am!"

CHAPTER 17

"i" to 'I' : Game of Gods

J UNIOR WAS RUNNING through a field of tulips, rows after rows of multicolored tulips with Sun setting behind his head making a halo around it. It appeared as if his feet were not touching the ground but gliding over it. He was moving so fast his body seemed to be scintillating light.

The camera man looking at him murmured softly "Of course Junior, you are supernatural, whether you accept it or not". He smiled. He knew as others did, that although Junior had not taken over the charge of the company, De Winter Enterprises stood rock solid on his unseen powers. He was cherished by all. Wherever he went he blasted one and all with his joy and love, and no one was immune to his laughing indigo eyes.

Soon Junior stood in front of the camera and as usual, he was grinning at the camera man. He asked "Should I sit on this wooden bench? What do you think? Or should I walk like a caged tiger, to and fro, in front of the camera?"

Camera man couldn't stop laughing. He replied, "Whatever you do Junior, don't become invisible again on the camera."

"No, of course not sir!" replied Junior.

"Junior, you know you have become invisible!"

"Am I? Really? Sorry, sorry." Junior said with an ear-to-ear grin.

"Okay, let us start." He said.

"You are already on, Junior."

"What? Oh, well then" He waved his hand at the unseen audience and asked "So, what are we talking about today? Something about love?"

He ran his fingers through his hair and remained silent for a short time. Then he said "No, not love. Today I am going to tell you a story, a legend. This legend is about our Divine Dreamer, the One Creator or if you prefer you can call it God. Hope you enjoy it.

Imagine it. Imagine the scene. Our hero, God, the limitless Creator, has limitless energy, with limitless possibilities to mold, to create something, anything, absolutely anything! And, of course whatever is created, it would be perfect, perfect to the last dot. God does not make mistake. God does not make junk. And this power is available to him eons after eons after eons. Does it sound a little monotonous, even boring? Imagine the same process goes on endlessly, with not even a challenge to alleviate the boredom. No challenge to overcome, because nothing goes wrong, ever! Perfect result every time!"

Junior looked at the camera man and burst out laughing. He said "What do you think? Won't it be deadly boring? No timeline to meet, nothing to master, no purpose to achieve! Just mindlessly being a creator, eons after eons after eons!"

Junior grinned and said "wait! Afterall there was a fly in the ointment! Our hero had to 'desire' something for the limitless energy field to create. But our hero had everything. So, what could he desire? Just imagine for a second what would you desire if you already had everything!"

Junior continued "Ah, but our hero, our one Creator is the brilliant one, intelligent, quite beyond comprehension of our logical mind. So, He came up with a game, a game to play, the 'Game of Gods'."

Junior paused for a few seconds, dragged his fingers through his thick hair and began "So then, how do you play this game? You play it in 3D as a virtual game which gives an illusion of a physical world consisting of light and dark, of good and bad, and, accessed by your senses. This was the perfect solution to get out of the ennui of continued sameness.

Now then, a 'mind' had to be created to play this virtual reality game in place of the True Self. I gave this 'mind' the name of little 'i'. Allow me to tell you some of the characteristics of this little 'i'. It is just a thought form made of human ego or your conscious analytical mind to play the game. It does not have a separate entity of its own. It tells a story about itself which goes something like this–'I am john Smith, I am male, I am an engineer, I am rich, I have million dollars, I own this car, I live in that house, I have to work hard to achieve success, I am this physical body, my body deteriorates as I age, I need to take medicines to keep this body healthy etc. etc.. He believes the quality of his life depends on outer circumstances. He thinks there is only one kind of power he can have, that is the physical power, power he may win by competing and defeating others, by subjugating and controlling others in some way, in short, mostly by infringing on others freedom, if he didn't want to be a victim to others' manipulations."

"Now the stage is set. The little 'i' has taken the place of your True Self, the big 'I'. It will desire things and Quantum Field will create it for it. The game began and you started enjoying different experiences with different desires with different characters you chose to play." Said Junior with a grin.

Junior looked around and continued with his usual laugh "It was the perfect plan to enjoy the game of life and to keep expanding our universe with ever new experiences. But alas it did not work out that way for long.

You see, the conscious ego mind was completely disconnected with the True Self, the big 'I'. It did not know the power of its own thoughts, beliefs and feelings. The little 'i' ruled them and lead them from the head believing everyone had to struggle and work hard to succeed. It didn't know the magnetic power of love which was in its very own heart with all the power to create their own dreams at will! Humanity felt like victims of someone or something, out there with more physical power. The reign of fear began. They felt they had no control over their lives. They were drowning in hopelessness. Pessimism was rampant. They lived in lack, lack of health, wealth and happiness, because they didn't know lack couldn't exist in our abundant universe. To free themselves from lack, they started stealing from others, which lead to fight, conflict, wars and chaos. And thus, you can see how the era of human suffering dawned on this beautiful planet."

Junior paused and ran his fingers through his hair and grinned at the camera man.

He began "Human suffering was not meant to be but for humanity's ignorance of their own inherent power. So, what began as a game for fun, for enjoyment, turned into a tragedy!

Junior laughed out loud and asked the unseen audience "This is the story of humanity, 'The Game of Gods' they have been playing.

But they have a choice. They can either continue playing the game of suffering lack, conflict and wars, or they can go all out to consciously reconnect with the big 'I', your True Self, the source of your power!"

Junior grinned and kept looking at the camera as if he could read the minds of the unseen audience. Then he asked "So, what do you think? What should humanity do? Alright, we will meet next week and find out. So long...see you."

He waved his hands and ran out of the range of the camera.

CHAPTER 18

But What If...

B RIAN AND MARK were sitting in the library discussing what to do with the mansions Junior had inherited from his grand-parents and parents. Just then they heard the piano playing. Mark said with a smile "Oh, Junior is back home. I love to hear him play. He creates new tunes like Gladiator did. Somehow it touches your heart."

Brian nodded his head and said "Yes. You know Mark, even now I miss Maxim, and I miss him more when I see Junior or hear Junior play piano or guitar like he used to."

Mark murmured "For me Gladiator and Alaska are living through him. That is how I perceive Junior and that makes me love him more."

After that they remained silent enjoying the music Junior was creating. After a minute or so Brian said, "Let us go to the music room and watch him play."

They went there and sat on the sofa to enjoy the music. Junior smiled at them and kept on playing. After a little while he stopped playing and said "I had better talk to Juliana. She has called me three times in past six minutes!"

Junior grinned and called her.

As she picked up the phone she asked "Where were you Blue? I called three times……"

"Yes, in six minutes! Where is the fire witch?" he laughed.

"Don't call me witch. I am not a witch. You see there is this boy in my class…" she began.

"Of course, there always is a boy, isn't there?" he grinned.

"Blue, are you going to help me or make fun of me?" she asked.

Junior laughed and said "Okay, okay, tell me how I can help you."

"Hmm..as I was saying there is this boy in my class who has a question. He is a nice boy, so I want to help him. You see we have formed a group of students who are interested in spiritual teachings. We all follow your spiritual school. We have watched the videos and holographic presentation of Gladiator. They are soooo…good. The thing is that this boy says he doesn't understand what we talk about. He doesn't understand spirit or spirituality. He doesn't understand how he can create his dream world out of nothing without struggling and working hard for it. I told him he should study the books and learn to meditate as advised by the spiritual school. He looked disappointed and said it was not for him. He believes he doesn't have the special quality or talent needed to become a successful creator. He promised he will keep trying but what if he couldn't do it? Isn't there a short cut, or some simple process that could help him to succeed in creating his desired life? That is the question Blue. Is there any way?"

"Sure, there is! Ask him to feel good, all the time. Feel excited, thrilled with life! Feel like singing, dancing, soaring high in the sky. He must maintain feeling good, for any reason, as much as possible, if not all the time. That is the short cut to success Juliana."

"Really?" Juliana asked.

"Yes. But tell him he must learn to ignore what is happening around him, if it does not make him feel good. He must transcend the physical reality that he sees around him otherwise he will get sucked in the misery of the collective, misery of the people, family, friends around him and will lose the 'feeling good' short cut to success. Yes, he must cultivate the knack of thinking, and feeling good all the time, for whatever reason, despite the suffering he sees in the world.

And ask him to smile. I mean smile more often. You see Juliana, when you smile, you are telling your sub-conscious that all is well, and thus, without doing anything you would have raised your vibration to match it to your dream world."

Junior paused. Juliana asked "Can it be done? Is it possible?"

Junior replied "Yes, it is very much possible. Tell your friend and ask him to report how he fares with the process. I have told you the pitfall he needs to avoid. If need be, he must defy the unhappy circumstances around him and keep feeling good. That is the trick."

Juliana thought for a second, then said "Okay. I will tell him. Thanks. Oh, wait! When are you coming to Boston? You promised!"

"Did I? No, I didn't promise. I said, 'trust me'. That is not the same thing."

"So, you want to wriggle out of coming to Boston? I wanted you to come Blue. I wanted you to show me how you took my pen. And so many other things as well." Juliana replied softly.

Junior asked, "You want me to come to Boston?"

Juliana said "Yes, that is what I said."

Junior said "So, that is your desire. You know what your Gladiator said–your desire gets fulfilled just by desiring it! So, you only need to desire your desire for it to come to fruition! It will, Juliana, if you do not doubt it. Never doubt your own power to create things out of thin air."

Juliana looked confused and said, "Yes, but if you don't want to come to Boston......."

Junior said "Where does my wanting come into the picture? You are the creator. It is your desire, and if you do not doubt, it will come to pass!"

"Really? You are sure?" asked Juliana.

Junior laughed and said "Ask your mother. In their college days they used to chase Gladiator. They went to schools, to Gyms, to airports to catch him and to ask him their questions. But poor things, they rarely could, because they doubted if they could meet him, while Alaska, my mother, stood by the door, with no doubts what-so-ever that Gladiator would find her and he did, every time."

Juliana was thrilled with this information. With her green eyes round like saucers, she exclaimed "Hey Blue, just you wait, I will have you in Boston soon, very soon!" and she laughed. Junior grinned to see her so excited and finally burst out laughing with her while Mark and Brian looked at each other and smiled.

CHAPTER 19

How to Use the Power of Love: Your Options

JUNIOR WAS STANDING alone under the round spotlight on the stage in the school's auditorium. He was silent for some time and then waved his hands and said "Today I am standing in our school auditorium in front of my teachers because they insisted that I share our talks with them. Yes, they are my teachers, each one unique and I love them. I am grateful to each one of them because they unstintingly showered me with their uncommon knowledge, and they embraced me to their hearts with unimaginable love."

Junior closed his eyes and stood silent on the stage.

After a short time, he opened his eyes, looked around with his laughing eyes and said "So, here I am to continue our discussion of last week. You know you are non-physical beings. You know you are the creator of your 3D reality. Now is the time for you to choose how you want to play this game of life. What are the options available to you? Let us find out."

He said "First option: You let the little 'i' to lead from your head believing in perceived physical reality as the truth.

You continue as you are, satisfied with your life interspersed with work, struggle, competition, conflict, sickness, helplessness. You choose this option because you prefer to remain in your known way of life. You might complain, blame, fight and suffer as a victim of the circumstances during the so-called bad periods, but all the same, you prefer to continue with this way of life. It is your comfort zone. It is your choice."

Junior paused for a few seconds. Then with his usual grin he started "Second option: You have heard about the spiritual truth that you are the creator of your reality. You want to experiment with it. You start practicing it. It is said you create your desired reality with your thoughts, your imagination, your beliefs and your feelings. So, you do your best, but you rarely get consistent result. Sometimes it works but other times it doesn't. You are disappointed and get disheartened. You think it is not for you or even that you are not good enough for your desire to manifest. And sad to say, but most people, at this stage, revert to option one instead of moving on to option three."

Junior stopped and ran his fingers through his hair as he did when in deep thought.

Then he looked up at the audience and began with a dazzling smile "Now we come to the third option. So, what is this third option: Besides knowing that you are the creator of your reality you also know that your universe is made of energy, with the possibility of molding itself to anything you desire. So, when you are thinking of creating your dream world, your goal, you need to feel the joy in your heart before your goal has manifested in physical reality. Feeling is the most important part of the process. You feel joy only when you have raised the frequency of your vibration to match the frequency of the thing you desire to manifest. You see, the Field of energy reads your vibration and based on it, it delivers your desired goods to you."

Junior paused, smiled at his audience and continued "There are three points in this process to note.

First: You must feel the joy of achieving your desire, before it has, in physical reality.

Second: You usually need to raise your vibration to the frequency of love or joy or gratitude to be able to manifest something good.

Third: Be aware of negative thoughts and beliefs. You cannot indulge in them because they lower your vibration. Yes, to be powerful creator you must maintain a high frequency of vibration of elevated emotions like love, joy, gratitude. If you remember, Gladiator said raise your vibration to the frequency of love, the frequency of your True Self and then, fearlessly create the world of your dreams.

You see, all these are examples of how to use the 'power of love' in your day-to-day life."

Junior smiled at his audience and said "There are other options and other ways to play the game of life. Enjoy experimenting with new processes and I would appreciate if you would share it with me."

After a pause he said "That is all for now. Take care. You are here to play the game and enjoy the experiences. That is the truth. Believe me." Saying so he waved his hand and walked off the stage.

CHAPTER 20

Mark Had a Suggestion

THEY HAD JUST finished dinner. Mark asked Junior "So, you completed your talks today. You explained what you learned from your parents."

Junior replied thoughtfully "Yes and no. Yes, I answered their 3 questions, that is, 'what is love', then 'why love' and the last 'how to use this love' in their daily lives. These were the three question they had asked me when I told them that I learned 'love' from my parents.

And no, I don't think they could have understood from my talks what I learned from Mom and Dad. Mark, it is quite complicated or rather, complex to put into words the truths about our one Creator and the creation."

Brian who was listening to their conversation commented "Even if Junior did explain it, I don't think it will be of any use to them. Do you think their logical mind will easily grasp the notion of having a non-physical boundless omnipresent Awareness?"

Mark answered "No, not easily, that is true. But if Junior could explain a little about our Creator and creation in simple terms it might awaken a desire, a curiosity in people to learn more about it. What do you think, son? Would you like to give it a try? Would you?"

Junior laughed at that and said "Let me think how I can do it. You know Mom and Dad rarely, if ever, gave me verbal instructions on the workings of our Creation. Putting the essence of spirituality into words will take some serious thinking. You see they never told me God and 'love' are one and the same. But I got it by watching both in action, so to speak. Both are like endless empty open cherishing space embracing every experience, so to say, with loving gratitude. No judgement, no resistance, no rejection, just a blissful oneness of all."

Brian said "Junior let me know when you plan to give this talk. I haven't heard you for quite some time. I want to be there for this talk."

Junior grinned and said "Are you sure Brian? Won't you get bored with this spiritual talk?"

Brian laughed and replied "Spirituality might bore me, but not you. You exude a kind of joyful energy that amazes me, that makes me come alive, as it does everyone else too."

Mark said "I will let you know, Brian. We will go together to watch our Junior speak." And Junior laughed.

CHAPTER 21

Blessings From Alaska and Maxim De Winter

J UNIOR WAS SITTING in front of the big mahogany table his father had used in the office of De Winter Enterprises. He was grinning from ear to ear radiating a joy filled energy which was palpable to one and all.

He began "In the seminar when I met you for the first time, you had asked me to share the spiritual knowledge I was privileged to receive from my brilliant parents. I had summed it up for you in one word 'love' and went on to explain 'what is love', then 'why love' and finally 'how to use this 'love', as I was asked by you that day. But you see my parents never gave me verbal instructions on spiritual truths.

I think you all know Mark. He is one of my guardians. He suggested that I should, at least, give you the basic essence of my parents' teachings, as I understood. What follows is some of the knowledge I imbibed from them.

After pausing for a second Junior continued "So, here I am sitting in my father's chair, feeling his vibration, ready to share his and my mother's spiritual understanding, share with anyone who is interested in learning it."

He began "I understood I am an extension of our one Creator. I am not separate from It. I am made of the same god stuff, the non-physical boundless Awareness and as such, I have the same powers. My natural state of being is that of 'love', and so, naturally I vibrate at the frequency of love. I am eternal non-physical being (like our Creator) having a physical experience. I have a physical body, but I am not it.

I understood this was the answer to the question 'Who am I?'. I was quite surprised to know that people didn't believe this spiritual truth! For them, I think, God is out there, somewhere, out of reach of us humans and only good for worshiping and praying.

But I know, my True self, that I call the big 'I', is the extension, a part, of the Creator. It is truly Me, who brought me into existence. I am a part of it, so it is natural for me to have a desire to know more of this unknown Dreamer, this unknown Creator. I think, it is my duty to reach out to It. And I also know it is quite easy for me to remain aware of this non-physical Self 24/7, if I wished to do so."

Junior thought for a few seconds and then continued with a smile "Furthermore, I understood, if for any reason, I got disconnected from my True Self, that I call the big 'I', I will lose my bliss, my joy, for then, I won't be vibrating at the frequency of love, the frequency of my True self. The pain of this separation from the big 'I' starts the suffering. Suffering is the creation of thoughts in the analytical mind, that I call the little 'i'."

Junior ran his fingers through his hair and said "So, in short, the first blessing, I received from my loving parents was to remain consciously aware of my non-physical Self, the big 'I', who I truly am. In truth, it is my default setting, so to speak, vibrating at the frequency of 'love'.

They literally anchored me into it."

Junior paused for a second and then said grinning broadly "You might be wondering why I brought you here to my father's office. Well, I want to show you my second blessing that I received from them. It is this painting of my mother, Alaska de Winter, done by my father Maxim de Winter, himself. This painting is alive although my mother is no more in this physical realm. I only need to look at it and I am engulfed in her unconditional love, her true essence. Did you know that she always radiated love? Wherever she went people got transformed by her loving presence!"

The camera moved to the life size painting of Alaska de Winter in front of the table where Junior was sitting and remained focused on it.

ABOUT THE AUTHOR

Alcyoné Sumila Starr, a science graduate, loves spirituality and all things esoteric. After years of research and meditation, she writes to demystify basic universal laws to bring hope, harmony and happiness to humanity in the most natural and effortless way. Her mission is to inspire, awaken and acquaint people with their own inherent power to create and to live the life of their dreams.

Furthermore, she confirms the secret of living a happy life, free from suffering, is to be aware of your non-physical True self and committing to perceive the world through a lens of unconditional love.

Contrary to the common belief, she adds, it is easy to maintain a conscious awareness of your non-physical True Self, the big 'I' or the 'I AM' or the 'Presence' or whatever name you choose to give IT!

She has participated in an international conference held in Brasilia, Brazil. She had presented a paper titled Civilian Capacity Building: The Spiritual Dimension, which was published as an annexure in the book titled "Civilian Capacity Building for Peace Operations in the Changing World Order".

She has written articles and books mainly on Spirituality. Her article "Building Bridges: A spiritual Approach" was published by Fair Observer–http://www.fairobserver.com/culture/building-bridges-spiritual-approach/.

She welcomes questions from her readers. She can be reached through her blogs on her website :

AlcyoneSumilaStarr.com

And by email at shikamesh@gmail.com
And on her facebook page.

ALSO BY ALCYONÉ SUMILA STARR

YOU ARE THE ULTIMATE MAGICIAN:
Fearlessly create the life of your dreams.

YOU ARE THE ULTIMATE MAGICIAN:
Know thy power and be free Book 2.

YOU ARE THE ULTIMATE MAGICIAN:
Love-the final frontier. Book 3.